Table of Contents

Kujichagulia Villages: A Practical Plan for Self-Determination

"Kujichagulia – Self-Determination: To define ourselves, name ourselves, create for ourselves and speak for ourselves."

– from the creator of Kwanzaa

Adinkrahene - Symbol for Greatness, Charisma and Leadership

Preface to the 2017 Edition

Gye Nyame - Fear Nothing but the Almighty Creator

It has been four years since first publication of this book. Much has changed and transpired over this time. The fate and destiny of Blacks within the U.S., Europe, Caribbean, Africa and throughout the globe has shifted, yet certain basic problems affecting the group have stubbornly persisted. New challenges have appeared as well as numerous opportunities for our group to gain advantages within the rapidly-shifting, technology-driven global economic order.

I have found the information within this book to be of immense value when explaining many of these changes that we are witnessing today. This information has received many compliments for its precise insights, practicality of actions, attention to areas too-often neglected, and for just being one solidly grounded plan for action. I have appreciated the compliments that have been extended.

Still, in the end the bottom line is change and transformation. As such, I can't help but feel that not nearly enough has been accomplished. In those areas where momentum toward the *Kujichagulia Villages* had been achieved in earlier years, the appearance of a devastating economic recession has taken much of the wind out of our sails. The funds for engaging village building have largely been diverted elsewhere.

Much of our previous momentum came from our Living In Black social media network, which had been a major force for our efforts. In the 9 years that have followed our initial efforts, Facebook and other social media networks have had a devastating impact on our LIB unity and sense of common purpose. Our members left us in droves for the convenience of FB's "Like" button and the thrill of posing as social media stars. It would have been hard to predict just how these new social media outlets would have taken so much from our global family which peaked at about 8500 registered members before dissolving into oblivion. I shut down Living In Black in 2016 due to lack of response from its members.

The nation has sunk to a new political, social and economic low in the aftermath of the recession. Eight years of the Obama presidency seemed to have lulled many activists into slumber. On a broad spectrum of fronts, Afri-Amers (African Americans) have lost ground and become subject to a whole new set of stresses. Today our group is beset by a spectrum of challenges, some of which are articulated throughout this book, and some have worsened in the past decade.

To the contrary, the world is turning and new empires steadily rising to displace the old and decaying. Change is good and so we welcome these new frontiers. The theme of "Africa Rising" had been in evidence a decade ago but has become more solidly established as a powerful global trend as the years go by. Where we reported phenomenal growth in the wealth of certain African oil-producing countries before 2010, today a new set of rapidly growing economies have appeared on the scene.

There is much to be excited about regarding the future ahead. Since this book was first published, I have consolidated my role as a "scientific futurist," and as such I can see transformation much more clearly now and in real time. The earliest chapters of Kujichagulia *Villages* tend to lean more heavily on the challenges that we face – challenges which are forcing our group toward deliberate processes for remedy. At a point in the book, the tone changes and it's all about practical solutions from then on. This is what I want my readers to get excited about.

I am proud to re-present this book to a new and broader audience. I think you will agree that there is great reason to be excited and optimistic about the future ahead as we consolidate sustainable development on a global basis. Africa Rising…WE got next!

We Commit to Self-Determined Reparations

Osram ne Nsoromma - Symbol of A New Beginning

I've been divinely blessed to have been involved with startup and preexisting rural development projects since I was a very small child in rural Ohio. Within the past decade, beginning in 2008, many of the members of our *Living In Black* social network along with other associates have generously supported and actively participated in my ongoing vision toward developing this vision of returning to and developing rural homesteads. Regarding four ongoing projects in Virginia, Louisiana, South Carolina and Illinois, we have hosted camping retreats, constructed facilities, planted gardens and orchards, brought in multiple resources, provided valuable labor, much needed capital and promotional efforts to raise awareness of these initiatives, further raising the founders' initial vision from that of farming to village building.

We are not new to this set of endeavors yet we feel compelled to raise the intensity of our involvement because of urgent and timely political, social and economic changes within the larger society. The rapid pace of these changes raises serious concerns regarding our collective security and compels us to immediate and sustained action.

We strive to *recover, repair and rejuvenate* a large part of our people's global position, resource management, land development and human resource potential. All of this amounts to self-determined "Reparations," a word which has come to symbolize the complete restoration of a people toward their historical greatness; in essence, it encompasses *The Repairing*. According to over a century of Reparations work from many organizations and individuals, this requires recovery, repair and rejuvenation in 9 major areas of our collective status:

1.   Compensation for Stolen Labor

2.   Land Recovery and Development

3.   Family and Community Redevelopment

4.   Economic Development & Business Expansion

5.   Education and Vocational Training

6.   Revising our Historical Perspective

7.   Rebuilding Our Transnational Relationships

8.   Repairing our Mental and Physical Health Status

9.   Overcoming the Impact of Injustice and the Criminal-Industrial Complex

There is a Pressing Need to Separate from the Cities

Fawohodie - Symbol of Independence

A truly history-changing wave of rural to urban migration of African Americans took place from the beginning of the 20th Century. Seeking to find refuge from the brutality of an American *apartheid* which was called Jim Crow, an estimated half million Blacks left southern states during the First World War and relocated to industrial centers such as Chicago, Detroit, Cleveland, Pittsburg, New York, Washington, Baltimore, Philadelphia and countless other cities large and small. Another wave followed the Great Depression and expanded again when the industrial labor demands of the Second World War compelled many more to join the northward migration.

The primary reasons for this migration were economic advantage, security, unrestricted access to educational resources and the right to organize ourselves without violent restriction toward political empowerment. For anyone who has knowledge of the conditions that southern Blacks suffered through for more than a century after Emancipation, we can certainly see how apartheid in southern states would compel them to seek an alternative and risk all by migrating away from lands that they had known for multiple generations.

Within recent years and especially currently, there has risen an intense debate about guns, defending ourselves, households and our land. All sides certainly agree that land is ultimately a collective investment which must be protected. Guns are best used to defend the commons; those lands and resources that are shared among large groups. Thus, when the media points our attention to the massacre of two dozen children and their teachers as took place in Sandy Hook, Connecticut, people should be rightly outraged and demanding of some alternate course for the nation's development.

Yet, what of the hundreds of young Blacks (and their teachers) killed within every one of America's largest cities each year for decades? Why does there seem to be a lack of national outrage and urgent efforts to put meaningful solution into place? Does America have selective blinders to the misery of Africans compared to everyone else? Should we reasonably expect that the government agencies should take care of this issue which hurts our own people so much when these same government agencies have such a long record of overlooking our people's fundamental need for security, economy, freedom and dignity?

Something profoundly historical is occurring as American has entered the 21st Century which we had better be aware of. We are witnessing for the first time in our development since the end of Jim Crow apartheid to status of children not achieving the quality of life of their parents. Comparing the inter-generational status of 1) the Great Generation, 2) Baby Boomers, 3) Generation X, and 4) The Millenials, we are witnessing a *degeneration* and *decline* in health, educational achievement and wealth transfer. This degeneration is measurable, widespread and totally unsustainable even for another four generations. Further, since the legalization of abortion in 1973, American Blacks have become the greatest *terrorists* in the destruction of our population and family. Despite so many positive advances over so many areas, we have done so while sacrificing a third of our population to uncertainty, selfish expediency and moral corruption initiated through foreign cultural values.

Why Did Our Forefathers Leave the Land?

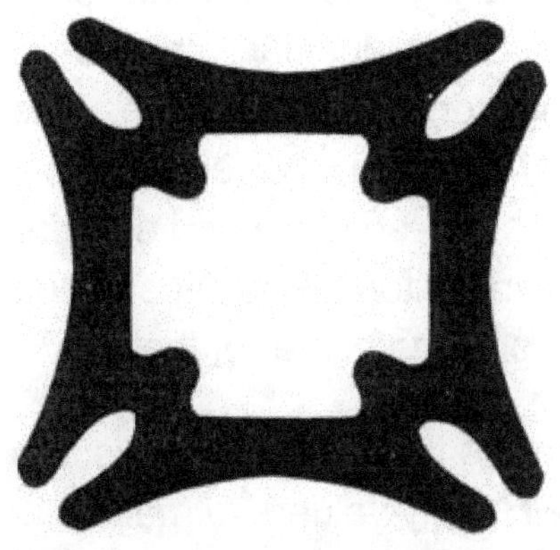

Fihankra - Symbol of Compound or Home

Our parents, grandparents and their parents left rural land bases and migrated to the cities to provide a better life for themselves and their families. They had lived on these lands for ten generations, emerging from the worst of the *Maafa, the Great Suffering* of enslavement. They left the South, emigrating from countless places where they suffered physical and psychic brutalization and invested their generation into making it better for future generations. To those who migrated we are immensely and forever grateful for their courage, moral conviction and dutiful work.

My own father was the 9th child of North Carolina sharecroppers who migrated first to West Virginia then onto Columbus, Ohio, in the decade following the Second World War. After serving during the Korean War he entered college in West Virginia, achieved a degree in chemistry and spent the rest of his career working as an industrial chemist in a large manufacturing corporation in Ohio. His compelling story is one of a million who followed the footsteps of his people who looked north and envisioned freedom and dignity, not just for themselves but for the families which would form the center of their social world.

They left to utilize their wisdom, skills, craft and labor, which were all highly valued, to make a better way for their children and future generations. They brought skills, a solid work ethic, craftsmanship, domestic management experience, artistic talents and much more to their new urban existence in the North. In the decades that followed this great migration our people became concentrated to the point that today 80% of our population is residing in these urban concentrations. Yes, we are *residing* in these large metropolitan areas but are we truly *living* within these concentrated areas?

Something Happened to the Metropolitan Industrial Base

Aya - Symbol of Endurance and Resourcefulness

Our people left the rural areas to feel more secure, to earn a decent living and to educate the children to an even greater earning potential. Tragically, it all started turning around after several generations. Through the Civil Rights challenges and a series of hard-fought victories from 1954 through 1965, we gained numerous advantages in politics, economics, justice and social structure. Yet, shockingly, things went awry after explosive riots signaled an impending cap to our *seemingly* unrestricted ascendance toward urban prosperity and social equality. Those who had in previous generations left the South as itinerant farmers had been able to lift the entire family up because of their dedicated labor and newly acquired education. By the beginning of the 1970's we began to witness signs that the road ahead would be filled with new struggles, many of which our leadership was completely unprepared to comprehend.

At a time when we felt so completely free, confident and secure within our hard-fought economic participation within America's industrial economy, subtle changes were organizing to envelop many of us within a whirlpool of damaging national trends that would sap our ethnicity of many of its cultural strengths, talents and resources. Because so many of us were drunk on the pride which the previous generation had struggled to return to our group, we did not pay attention to the new behaviors and indulgences which would usher in a set of degenerate trends that have now shown to have destroyed much of our group potential.

What happened when the economic base collapsed?

Where did the steel mills go? What happened to the huge industrial base that kept our laborers occupied? The U.S. used to be world leader in the manufacture of televisions, refrigerators, appliances and most other consumer goods. Over the course of the decades of the 1980's through the first decade of the 21st Century, those manufacturing facilities along with their huge labor needs were shipped overseas largely due to the greed and avarice on the part of the directors of profit-driven corporations.

Left behind were collapsed economic bases and, subsequently, increasingly desperate living on the part of the abandoned labor force. A new, illicit economy took the place of the manufacturing labor economy that our parents relied upon. How did the drugs get from distant locations into these urban areas? The oligarchy controlled all the mechanisms by which the new urban drug economy would take over our communities and redirect our youth into participation. The so-called "Drug War" failed many years ago. It did succeed in turning sick and abandoned people into fodder for the prison industrial complex. It was a covert *eugenics* program and now our people are bearing witness to its ultimate outcome.

Feminism took hold of many cultural values which were needed to sustain our own ethnicity's distinct historical development. Due to several trends, to too great an extent, the black man was pushed further and further away from the center of family and community in absolute contradiction to his historical position as provider, protector and leader of critical group-centered needs.

Television, Hollywood cinema, disco and other means of leisure time engagement corrupted our morals and intellect on vast scale. We were systematically lead by the hidden hand of social engineers into become a separate and detached demographic element within America, sometimes openly referred to as "the unassimilated immigrants", "redundant labor", "disenfranchised urban youth", and worst of all "useless eaters."

Blacks were first *forcefully immigrated* into the United States as a source of cheap and inexhaustible labor. For the better part of nearly 20 generations we were valued because of our labor, skills, resilience and will to self-sacrifice. Things have turned for the worse and for the first time since Emancipation our children have inherited a culture which is making them physically weaker, less educated and poorer.

Current trends are further feeding this downward spiral. The promise of *hope* which accompanied the election of an African American president Barack Obama had become shattered with the realization as of his reelection that he really has no intention of engaging in the myriad of processes which serve to recover, restore and repair this damaged segment of the national population. He kept to his stated 2008 campaign position of NOT supporting Reparations for Blacks in America. The catastrophic impact of the national recession redirected at least a quarter of a billion dollars from real estate equity for African Americans; that money was directed to satisfy trillions of dollars of usury, profiting a people who had zero concern for our long-term destiny. An out of control national debt has now forced austerity and structural adjustment programs on the economy that is disproportionately affecting our economic community.

Our People Are Now Dying Off in the Cities

Hye Wonhye – Symbol for That Which Cannot Be Burnt

We've found a thousand innovative ways to die off in these cities. Marriage and childbearing rates have plunged and now Blacks in the U.S. have reached a *negative fertility rate*. Black men are excluded from the workforce in vast numbers *except* for the extremely low-compensated workforce rising within the nations prison industries. Our predicted rise to the top minority demographic which had been predicted by the middle 21st Century has reversed itself. Others are now regarded as the new rising minorities (Hispanics and Asians) and ours is regarded as a dying population. Our children are 25 times more likely to be injured by the toxic conditions and stress of urban living than they are from gun violence. They are dying from suicide, homicide, cancer, obesity-related disease (1 in 7 is now obese before elementary school), CVD, diabetes of the youth, and other psycho-social stress induced ailments.

The medical-pharmaceutical healthcare complex has become a major cause of death for Africans in the U.S. While there has been an immense (and justified) protest over recent years due to the shocking number of police homicides against our members, there has been little or no protest over the death toll from bad medicine. **Iatrogenics (death-by-doctor)** has become a major cause of premature death for all Americans. Annual rates of death for Blacks in the U.S. have reached as high as 170,000 – when iatrogenic death is compared to police homicides in 2016, this stands as a stunning ratio of 425-to-1.

Many of us have lost our psychological and spiritual grounding in this unstable and stressful urban environment.

When we become so unstable in this environment we lose hope. We fall into fantasy and superstition. We are over-consuming junk media, "reality shows" and cultural garbage specifically packaged for urban African American consumption. Drugs and food fill the void of our spiritual emptiness and lack of "sweetness" in our lives. Relationships that held family together for generations are now so strained that many see us as our worst enemy.

The very institutions which held us together through the worst of the enslavement period have new become so damaged that they may appear unrecoverable. Raising a healthy family in the cities is increasingly difficult.

People are locking themselves into homes with barred windows like mini prisons. Gated communities are like larger confinement centers. Now talk is about putting armed guards into schools to protect from gun violence. New urban school structures already are being built with high walls, fences, high security and lighting that resembles low-security incarceration facilities. The "school to prison pipeline" is growing more apparent every decade. It is becoming increasingly difficult to raise healthy families. We have got to still believe in our potential to do what our parents and grandparents could do and to make things better for the next generation.

We will NOT benefit from putting more guns into schools. We need more, better and more relevant cultural education for our children. Our schools don't need to be turned into armed internment zones. Martial arts could be taught

Private armed security functions to protect certain populations. For home and business protection that is not such a bad idea. But how do we protect ourselves from substance abuse, educational failure and from being preyed upon by profit-driven corporations who only see us as unwitting consumers.

We must raise our children with a healthy self-image and appreciation of their own distinct ethnic and cultural heritage. Our youth must be taught, like other ethnic groups, to see their cultural inheritance as valuable and not subject to compromise. Like Persians, Chinese, Italians and other ethnic groups, through Kujichagulia / Self-Determination we can take responsibility toward developing our own community's economies and teaching our children to respect our culture for its true worthiness.

If we examine caste hierarchies within nations around the world we too often see the Africa as the lowest status throughout the globe. Even within our own African and Caribbean nations we are regarded lower in status than immigrants and sometimes even receive less thoughtful care than people's pets. We can and we must build upon models based upon our own, cultural values and wisdom. We need to develop a single process to repair a spectrum of persistent problems.

Notes on Social Engineering

Nkyinkyim - Twistin, Symbol of Initiative and Dynamism

We have tried and failed at praying a solution into process by petitioning to invisible deities. We must be more scientific and systematic in our approach. *Social Engineering* is the method by which the leaders of large structures redirect a people's resources and focus toward mass mobilization aimed at solving widespread problems affecting the group. Note the following very precise formula for social engineering:

> "Sufficient financial backing for regular utilization of mass media, constantly to communicate the desired objectives to the 'common man.' New values can be deliberately created, disseminated, and adopted as personal and collective goals highly desirable of achievement.

But the concerted effort of the major social institutions—particularly the educational, recreational, and religious—must be enlisted with the ready cooperation of those in control of the mass media… By utilizing the various tested devices, our modern genius in advertising may alight upon simple phrases well organized in sequence and timing, and coordinated with other efforts geared to realize the 'grand design.' But there are required a host of laborers with plenty of financial backing."

— Sociologist Philip J. Allen, Univ. of Virginia

This excerpt contains some 26 separate points which must be orchestrated together to make for a unified strategic program that will influence the lives of the group's members. These changes are intended to last for generations. Like a concert band, various critical segments of society must be guided by skilled intellect. These agencies include: 1) Financial backing, 2) education, 3) recreation, 4) religion and 5) mass media.

Unless and until we put such a social engineering process into place we run the risk of losing it all. Other civilizations have disappeared from history. We study the great historians who have brought us foundation of our successes and failures of the past. "What happened to the people of Sumer? They disappeared because they lost their history."

Tragically, too many of our group members within the U.S. are clueless as to who are such luminary historians as Cheikh Anta Diop, Chancellor Williams, Drusilla Dunjee Houston, John Henrick Clarke, Theophile Obinga, Ivan Van Sertima, Anthony Browder, Asa Hilliard, John G. Jackson, J.A. Rogers, Yosef ben-Jochannan, Marimba Ani and others who worked so hard to give us a world history past record that we could be amazingly proud of. I am presuming that you, because you have chosen to read this book, are not suffering from this history-literacy deficit. Still, beyond a small percentage of us that actually care whether our global historical record is being taught to our group members, does a sizeable percentage of our youth (or their parents for that matter) even have the slightest knowledge of who these great scholars are?

There is a Kenyan proverb which goes, "Until the lion learns to write, the tale of the hunt will always reflect the glories of the hunter." We must do a better job of informing our masses of the great historical record which our group members should hold dear as inheritance.

One of the important rules of social engineering is mastery of mass communications. We need to control such facilities to teach our people, inform them, ignite unified action, highlight opportunities and forge appropriate responses to security challenges.

Land Acquisition and Development

Sankofa - Symbol Meaning Go Back and Fetch

Land is not considered a renewable resource. Blacks haven't fully comprehended the impact of the 70% to 85% (according to differing accounts of farm acreage ownership) of our farmland that was disowned by African Americans during the 20th Century. Our forbearers worked so hard to acquire and develop this farmland. Their descendants did a very poor job of keeping, maintaining and developing the land for the wealth of theirs and future generations. According to research from the 1912 Edition of *The Negro*

Yearbook (as cited in the book *Desegregating the Dollar* by Robert E. Weems, Jr.), at the beginning of the 20th Century our appreciation of land acquisition and development was much more focused:

> It is estimated that the Negroes are adding each year to their wealth from $20,000,000 to $30,000,000. They now own about 20,000,000 acres of land or 31,000 square miles, an area almost equal to that of Vermont, New Hampshire, Massachusetts, Connecticut and Rhode Island… Negroes now own and operate 64 banks, 100 insurance companies, 300 drug stores and over 20,000 dry goods and grocery stores, and other industrial enterprises.

Churches, once the backbone institution to provide for the welfare of our people, have become something entirely different and are being led by individuals expressing markedly different values than those of their grandparents. According to research I've previously published (*Minister, Thou Art Bound: The Corruption of the Black Clergy in the U.S.*, 1998) throughout our history black churches served 14 critical functions that held our communities together. Today, some 80,000 black churches in the U.S. are the last widespread institutions still under exclusive control of black leadership. They still have immense resources and facilities which could be utilized toward our vision of self-determined Reparations. The major challenge with religious institutions stems from the low educational level and inconsistent values within the leadership. There are undoubtedly many outstanding leaders within these religious institutions yet the overall momentum is still going the wrong way.

One culturally-inspired church, the Shrine of the Black Madonna, with several urban chapels, has acquired some 5000 acres of rural land in South Carolina. Purchase of the Beulah Land Farms was part of a bold vision for empowerment of the group's visionary founder Jaramogi Abebe Agyeman (formally known as Albert B. Cleage, Jr.; 1911- 2000). Within recent years however, possession of the land is reportedly in danger because the 2nd generation of Shrine leadership disputed as to how to manage church assets, including the Beulah Land Farms.

Where is the vision which can be translated from generation to generation which can hold onto vast agricultural real estate holdings and make them work for our people's true and timely needs? We will continue to outreach and develop partnerships with church leadership. As frustrating as my own efforts have been over the years toward this outreach, we cannot allow this critical institution to slip away without negotiating its efforts to come forth toward self-determined Reparations. If it is strictly a matter of quid pro quo ($$$) somehow, we have got to convince religious leadership that we provide something that they need. Fresh organic produce and other crafts from our Kujichagulia Villages could be sold on church properties in farmers' markets. This could very well be an ideal bargaining chip to secure better long term economic collaboration.

There is a difference between *real* estate and mortgaged equity accumulation.

With the tremendous crash in the real estate market which signaled the end of the first decade of the 21st Century, a sizable percentage of households were swindled by a decades-long scheme cooked up by unscrupulous agents of *usury* that peaked in 2006 and came tumbling down by 2010. Under this disastrous scheme, many of us were conned into investing our families' wealth into extremely risky home mortgages. This con was organized by a collective of Wall Street "Banksters" and countless outlaws throughout the real estate and financial services sector. In the end, many of us were stunned; left with our pants down around our ankles and feeling horribly violated. We have now come to realize that we had been "played" for a significant portion of our financial future and our children's inheritance by economic "hit men"; a bunch of blood-sucking profiteers who were masters of slight-of-hand.

The calamity of unsustainable debt accumulation in the near-complete collapse of the urban economy has got to be fully comprehended by those who were *victim* to the theft of hundreds of billions of dollars by these Banksters' usury grab. In hindsight, we should *never* have bought into their "too-good-to-be-true" home equity confidence game in the first place. Credit cards, real estate mortgages, auto loans and leases, debt default hedges and complex investment instruments such as derivatives are *not* natural – they were generated through complex computer algorithms created by mathematical calculation. The mass of homeowners targeted by these Banksters were ripped off big time and many of our so-called leaders (including government regulatory agencies) appear to have been collaborators who benefited from the scheme.

It may take decades to fully comprehend the whole story of this massive hijacking of the wealth of the middle class's real estate trust. In a few words, we can determine that this serves as one of the greatest financial crimes in modern history. We must also note that very few of these *white-collar criminals* were punished. Consequently, we hold all levels of law enforcement and the judiciary in contempt for not upholding their sworn duty to protect us from these "Masters of Deception."

In a familiar pattern, paralleling the massive debt and real estate scam, the medical-pharmaceutical complex is currently perpetuating a massive fraud which is costing African Americans hundreds of billions of dollars annually in improper medical practices and procedures that borders on outright criminal fraud. They are plundering the larger U.S. economy for over $3 trillion annually while delivering a shockingly expensive healthcare system that, according to the World Health Organization, ranks only 41st on the scale of affordability and satisfaction when compared to 191 other nations around the world.

Meanwhile, a small handful of wealthy individuals are quietly buying up millions of acres of land.

Most people are completely oblivious to the concentration of huge tracts of America's farm real estate in the hands of a relatively small group of landlords. This modern feudalism is another of the many traps that have negatively impacted families through their own inattentiveness and unenlightened consumerism. John Malone and his business partner Ted Turner, along with a relatively small handful of other billionaires are investing in vast holdings of available acreage which can support agribusiness. Yet, there is no real obstacle blocking us from similarly organizing to acquire substantial farm properties. Numerous times I have researched online resources to examine what type of agricultural land is available in those areas of the country where our population is concentrated, especially the South. Some of these parcels are incredible deals. I remain puzzled as to why it is so difficult to motivate people to move on this land before the billionaires scoop it all up for themselves!

We can act now to reverse over a century of land loss. African American increased spending during the 90-day winter holiday shopping season, which can amount to between $40-$55 billion annually, is largely squandered on consumption which does little or nothing to change our destiny. A mere 5% to 10% of these monies could be used to purchase at least 700,000 acres per year, which over the course of a decade could make up for a century of farmland lost by African Americans. With a 10 percent redirection of this holiday shopping money, there would still be hundreds of millions of dollars remaining for developing these 700,000 acres.

We have got to become conscious of our distorted values and how cultural misdirection leaves us powerless and unable to secure our children's wealth destiny.

Where might we look to find good land for development? Just look south to where our people already live in large numbers and where our ancestral blood, sweat and tears was infused into the soil during the period of our enslavement within this country. Additionally, we could and should be looking to the Caribbean where our ancestral roots run deep. Ultimately, what we are doing should serve as models for repatriation efforts to return and build a mighty

African nation to its full self-determining potential. Sadly, as it is right now, powerful private groups from the U.S., European, Asian and Arab countries are quietly acquiring huge land holdings in Africa. African Americans are excluding themselves from helping to avert one of the biggest land grabs in modern history. The criminal schemes that plundered our families' wealth continue in another arena largely due to our inattention.

Yet once we have come to awareness of the importance of these trends, there is no reason for us to remain passive. We can begin to act immediately by acquiring land in Mississippi, Louisiana, Alabama, Georgia, North and South Carolina, Virginia as well as agricultural parcels in other states, such as Tennessee, Arkansas and elsewhere. We can even begin by acquiring distressed and abandoned urban plots and teaching ourselves and our children to grow organic foods and herbs. Additionally, it would be very easy to create a series of craft workshops where similar work could be quickly initiated. We can begin where we are with the resources that we already possess and control.

Calling Forth Concerned People with Skills and Resources

Akomo Ntoso – Symbol for Understanding and Agreement

There are significant economic, cultural and social divisions which have emerged within the nation and within our communities that undermine our group's ability to project its strength. Yet, strong common needs persist for clean water, wholesome food, sustainable economics, security, education for children, optimal health etc. It is our vision that within the controlled environment of Kujichagulia Villages, supported by binding connections to urban communities, we can significantly reduce the gap between securing that which we so badly need and that which has been in a downward spiral within recent generations.

Accordingly, the best way that we can accomplish this vision is by coordinating large numbers of talented and creative people to work together toward a transforming vision. Within the Villages we all learn to replicate the values which brought people together at the dawn of civilization where we share our surplus for economic freedom and security. That's how societies were formed and we must return to this pathway now to protect and defend ourselves from the increasingly hostile environments within these oversized cities. We can and must call on the values which our ancestors drew upon to create the very foundation for human civilization. Within the cultural development of African civilizations, we have and continue to develop these codes for guiding the behavior of the larger group. These include, among many others: the Nguzo Saba, Seven Principles of Ma'at, 10 Cardinal Virtues; 42 Positive Affirmations, the Adinkra, and many more.

In the aftermath of truly appreciable advances accomplished through the efforts previous generations, things have changed dramatically since the culmination of the era of the Civil Rights Struggle. Beginning with the so-called "Baby Boomers", subsequent generations have delayed for too long their obligation to commit to procedures for solving persistent problems and because of this negligence, we all suffer.

In previous generations our segregated communities contained nearly all the practical vocations needed for our survival. This self-sufficiency is where tribes and villages evolved from. Everything that was needed we found amongst ourselves or acquired through means by which the group could sustain trade. We grew food, protected the land, built homes, educated our youth, created marketplaces and provided highly-valued crafts for trade.

I was fortunate to have experienced this self-sufficiency personally as I grew up in such a setting whereby 21 black families, most with children, bought land from a retiring black farmer. Each homestead was developed upon from one to three acres of land and most contracted to build their own modern and stylish houses. We were an interdependent community and all children were cared for by every member of the block. All the elders on the block were respected by these children who were obligated to help the elders maintain their properties.

My father was an ideal role model for myself and three brothers to grow into competence, productivity and self-sufficiency. He was college educated, an industrial chemist, a single parent, skilled chef, gardener, community leader and educator at church as well as plumber, carpenter and vocational instructor, a hunter, fisherman and a spectrum of other *practical* skills he had gathered throughout his life. As well, he and other fathers on our block commonly shared a diverse set of skills, maintained strong marriage bonds, displayed high personal morals and values which most of the younger generation took upon us to emulate.

Today we must continue along this pathway to do our own part to recreate this historical transfer of freedom, dignity, and a culture of self-determination. Many of you can certainly relate to what I am sharing about my own root foundations because, like my brothers and me, you were raised in a comparable manner.

Youth Need to Be Guided Toward Viable Professions

Ananse Ntontan - Symbol for Wisdom and Knowledge

Youth are too often languishing in the cities. Their lives are endangered by a broad spectrum of challenges which were alien to previous generations. So many seem to be addicted to electronic umbilical cords (television, electronic gaming, social networking and "smart" media) and disconnected from interacting with the larger society in meaningful world matters. Too many are seemingly addicted to smart phones and to consumption patterns initiated by profiteers who are often using these youth like disposable commodities. Because of media brainwashing, they regularly consume toxic food and drink which has now burdened their generation with disease epidemics once considered to be "geriatric disorders" – associated with advanced aging.

How might we educate our youth practically; toward power and self-sufficiency? Public schools have been largely teaching most of our youth *social conformity*. They are taught to unconsciously serve the social designs of a caste hierarchy which benefits those at the top of the wealth structure. This caste system is based upon superficialities which are all too often reinforced by intentional exclusion (If you're white, you're right; If you're tan, you're the Man; If you're brown, stick around; If you're black, stay back!) Colorism, gender, height, educational certification, religion and wealth status are primary caste values which are subliminally and overtly pushed within this society.

Who might teach our sons, as did my own father, the craft of plumbing, whether at home or as a skilled profession? On average, plumbers make more money than lawyers. Won't the larger society continue to need carpenters, heavy machine operators, agriculturalists, media production, design and engineering? Can we do a better job of humanizing future generations than the corrupted values they are learning from mass media? They must acquire food preparation and culinary skills which will keep them and their families healthy.

At a certain point, it appears that fathers stopped teaching their sons and mothers ceased instructing their daughters in the fundamentals which bonded family and community together. Through Kujichagulia Villages we envision a whole new spectrum of vocations coming together to serve the critical needs of this time and the future. The U.S. Department of Energy Solar Decathlon stands as one example of the type of instruction that can bring a new reality within the emergent "Green Economy."   The Solar Decathlon is a bi-annual competition among dozens of universities across the U.S. and from around the world, where student engineers compete to design the future of solar powered, solar heated housing construction.

Because this DOE Solar Decathlon is sponsored in large part by federal money, we the taxpayers of this country, or any among us who can surf the Internet, have access to the architectural blueprints of these home models; I have been collecting them for years. We will begin using these blueprints toward construction of our own permanent housing at the Village sites.

Instructing the youth into a spectrum of traditions within the healing arts practices is another area where people of talent and skills must step forward. Based upon projections of the impact that 80 million Baby Boomers will have on the healthcare services, we should be rushing to get as many of our youth prepared as possible to prevent a huge proportion of our reported trillion-dollars-a-year Black consumer spending from falling into the hands of outsiders. These entities have no intention of repairing our illnesses or repatriating surplus profits back toward our distinct community needs.

We Are the Most Educated yet Dependent Group on Earth

Mate Masie - Symbol of Wisdom, Knowledge and Prudence

Africans in the Diaspora are the most educated and wealthy, yet dependent people to be examined. Black Americans have had so much access to libraries, media, higher education and electronically transmitted information, bank loans and other economic resources – especially compared to other Blacks. Yet so much of what we've learned is not put into practice and so much is unworthy of being practically applied. The so-called Baby Boom generation witnessed our best and saw it turn into the worst for this and subsequent generations. What we've inherited has now become unsustainable and is degrading our status backwards toward the values of Jim Crow apartheid. Too many current college graduates are merely prepared to seek J.O.B.S. (Just Over Broke Syndrome) and not to develop businesses for their own economic viability.

The word Kujichaguila (Self-Determination) expresses a value which can transform our dependency into a dynamic energy that will move us firmly toward a new destiny. This great access which history has afforded us has got to be translated into practical actions with predictable outcomes. Our people have first-hand experience in heavy industry, urban development, invention, arts and humanities, military management, managing large infrastructure assets (seaports, airports, transportation, banking and financial planning). These talents and experiences must be redirected to something capable of serving the *group self-interest*. Time is not expected to be kind to us if we delay forging the base for our own liberation. Each of us has a critical part to play in this Reparations process.

Predicted and unpredictable crises are arising yearly, and compound over decades, which negatively impact our position within society. We can certainly conclude that such challenges move us toward deliberate actions which serve to solve problems. Each of us must assume a key place in this transformation. Thus, we have been given the task by our forbearers to stay involved and to work for the long term self-interest of the group. Our passions and commitments have been forged from the fire within the hearts of those before us. We now transfer that fire to future generations.

We must stay ahead of the downsizing of the domestic workforce.

For the foreseeable future, the downsizing of the U.S. workforce is predicted to continue. A sizeable proportion of the nation's industrial jobs were exported in order to facilitate higher profits for the empowered oligarch. These jobs might never come back as strong as they were in the decades that followed World War II. Skilled and experienced workers are now struggling to find employment for a fraction of the wages they enjoyed earlier in life. At the same time, many U.S. industries are clamoring to bring in highly educated foreign workers to further displace our children's place in the workforce. The trend of globalization is still ongoing and the newly emergent *service economy* is hard pressed to serve the needs of the average American family. How can we then imagine that it will serve to the benefit of our youth?

Despite so many ways that the labor market has shifted from the impact of demographic changes stemming from abortion to immigration, for a large segment of millions of youth entering this stage of their adulthood, this trend is still degrading. Yet there will always be certain skills such as agriculture, teaching and healthcare, which will be necessary to sustain the population. Yet, with proper research and leadership, we can identify these macro-economic trends, stay steps ahead of labor shifts and allow each of our members a base for bartering their skills, talents and labor for a good living for themselves and their family.

Under national policies of austerity and structural adjustment, wages continue to move downward relative to the cost of living which is going up. We'd better come up with some sort of a strategic plan or else we will continue to experience this degradation which has been disproportionately impacting our community for decades.

In the climate of a broad downsizing of the labor force, we can still make sure that everyone has a valued place in the development of society. We can feed every member of our collective highly valued and healthy food produced through our own labors. We can educate each member of our group into skilled crafts that afford them a sense of pride, self-esteem and the satisfaction of their own accomplishment. We must assure that every child is surrounded by loving teachers which will guide them to productive adulthood wherein their characters are well-integrated. **Kujichagulia** means that we take primary responsibility for securing our own future.

Skilled Craftsmen Can Barter their Talents for Vital Commodities Needed for Survival

Denkym - Symbol of the Crocodile for Adaptability

When a person has highly valued skills, it is a guarantee that they are going to eat. We have identified a lengthy list of such skills, crafts and talents as well as means and methods to exchange them for the necessities of life. Within many *Intentional Communities* around the world alternative currencies are now being developed that can allow close-knit communities to exchange amongst their selves without having to always resort to the Yankee Dollar as *the* primary standard of value.

For example: Since the dawn of civilization African artwork was highly valued because it symbolized the essential spirit and foundation of our traditional cultures. Consequently, African art still trades for high value wherever it is marketed. New systems for value exchange will be critically needed for our growth and sustainable development apart from the current national system, which is dominated by corrupt practices of fabricated value, usury (loan sharking) and market manipulation.

By engaging in the process of homesteading we reacquire a spectrum of highly valued professional skills with which we can barter among ourselves.

If you were to do an online research on the word "homesteading" you may be surprised at the diversity of resources which are available. There are magazines, web sites, books, videos and campus resources which can be saved to your computer hard drive which can serve as blueprints for building our families' futures. This is what the families within the neighborhood of my youth all *practically* applied. We drew our own water from beneath the grounds upon which we built our own homes. We grew a large portion of our food and handcrafted many of the items which were practical instruments of daily living.

Today there is a robust new rural homesteading culture within the U.S. but too few of its participants are of African ancestry, although we are NOT completely excluded from the movement. There are ongoing successful models of us doing this which cannot be ignored. Fears that our efforts will be destroyed such as Rosewood, Tulsa Oklahoma, Colfax and other massacres should not preclude us from counting the vast number of successful communities we built. Beyond the horrible massacre which took place in 1921 in Tulsa, our people had managed to establish a total of 23 all black towns in Oklahoma, 13 of which still exist today. We've done this before and we can certainly do it again. Our own Living In Black family is currently building in partnerships in Illinois, Louisiana and Virginia. Several times a year I receive invitations to do the same Kujichagulia development in other locations as well.

Too many of our members have become so pessimistic that they simply cannot imagine that this could ever work. The need to simply attend one of the seasonal *Ujima Camping Retreats* at one of our ongoing projects to witness how wonderful it feels to become aware of how we can live, work and thrive together. Yes, we can be as capable as any other people at constructing a good life for ourselves and our children. One simply must witness firsthand the commonality and attraction to like-minded people, those whose cultural values best reflect our own. Our challenge is to bring witness to those whose imagination had yet to "imagine-a-nation" of our own.

We are calling visionary people forward to forge a new homesteading movement. We must consider that our villages could very well serve as "survival arks" to protect our youth and families from the perils that threaten to obliterate urban communities.

Building Political and Economic Sovereignty

Nkonsonkonson - Symbol for Unity and Community

On our own land, we govern ourselves and hold primary responsibility. We know our basic needs are for food, housing, security, education and governance. Naturally, security for all of this is too important to be ignored and history proves that we can defend that which truly hold in high regard. A couple of years back, on one of our Regional Ujima Camping Retreats, apparently some local hooligans were intent on playing games with us as we sat around the campfire enjoying our own company. Security-minded brothers (who had been engaging so many other duties without bring unneeded attention to their being armed) chased the "ghosts" away with authority (pow, pow, pow – 3 shots into the air). What was disturbing to me was that so many of our members responded like they had no idea at all how to respond. Fortunately, my small amount of training could get the women and children out of any potential harm until we had discovered the source of the loud pops as being from our own Brothers on Point.

Security concerns for Kujichagulia Villages are valid and must be taken seriously, just as it should be for every urban community. While our primary method of approach is to give the youth something that inspires them to positive social conformity, threats must be neutralized with quickness and authority. We are thus supportive of the right to bear arms as is stated in the Second Amendment and to the responsible training of our youth in firearms safety. If we are to protect our people at these Kujichagulia Villages, then we must also consider our people in Chicago, Detroit, New Orleans and the thirty cities where our people live in large numbers in America's cities. It is OUR responsibility to protect ourselves.

In a profit-driven capitalist nation, we must develop economic structures. We need food, housing, upkeep of our retired and elderly, systems of education and self-governance. We must tap the wisdom and experience of these highly accomplished and esteemed elders for the best interests of our future.

Our people know how to weave great fabrics in African villages that are now being copied in remote places in Asia and Europe, only to be exported back into the African countries from which their patterns were stolen.

In a money-driven capitalist nation we must develop autonomous means of capital development, acquisition and management. We must and will create our own needed structures. "Healthcare" in the U.S. is now costing about $10,000 per capita per year in 2017 for every person in the country when one considers all sources of payment. Could we formulate a plan to capture just *half of that* to invest in our rural healing retreats? Can we use our knowledge to reverse the ravages of high blood pressure, CDV, diabetes, obesity and other preventative areas? We can and will stop investing our children's inheritance in the medical-pharma complex and their profit-driven motivations. Even with a weekend camping retreat, or weeks at one of our villages, people can come up with a whole new definition of their healthy lifestyles.

After my first trip to Africa in 2006, where I spent over two weeks in Egypt, I returned to this country knowing that I was forever transformed and that my future activities would thereafter reflect the awesome historical legacy which I had been exposed to. It is our intention that many people will feel the same after visiting our little African villages.

Restoring Leadership to the Council of Elders

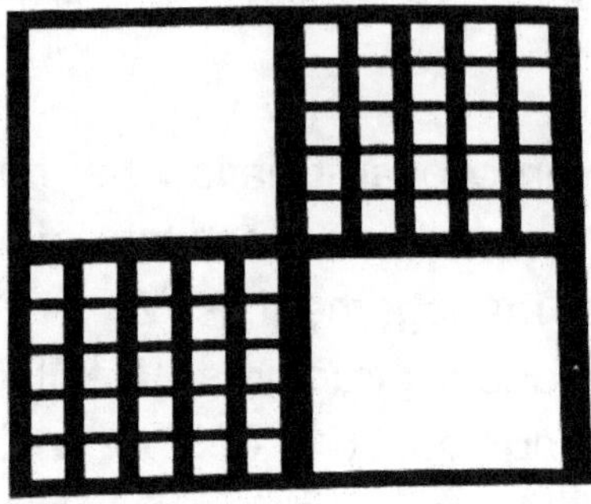

Kontire Ne Akwamu - Symbol for Democracy and Dialogue

The two-party political structure that dominates the American political economy has failed to adequately attend to our group's self-interests.

Democrats have long held majority control over big city school boards that have greatly damaged educational opportunity for urban youth. Republicans have disproportionately controlled industries that have excluded these youths and their parents from enjoying economic advantage and opportunity. Despite a myriad of leadership faults, there is no reason to place disproportionate blame on President Obama for the grand failure of the nation's wealthy who have developed a system which excludes us; he's late to a party which was well underway before he stumbled into it.

The American population has been increasingly bankrupted for decades before the failed Healthcare Reform Act of 2010 was passed that entrenches the current failing system of expensive disease management. Our need is for preventative healthcare and our Kujichagulia Villages will be the ideal way for a family of four, currently spending over $700 per week for bad healthcare, to create a new wellness lifestyle and save half the money for investment in other parts of their development.

To restore ourselves to a path of sustainability, we must give disproportionate direction and control to our wise and esteemed elders. We must take care of them the way that they have always taken care of us when they are in need. We can shore up this crumbling social security network with our rural collectives. Our parents are being forced to work far beyond retirement age, up until the time that their health fails, in this current system. We must learn to homestead, grow our own, take care of our children and elders and empower those in our community who are the natural leaders.

True democracy means that everyone can have a voice for decisions regarding the Commons. We can go forward by going back to these values (Sankofa). Politics in the U.S. are now producing billion-dollar election campaigns. We cannot be players in such an environment. Yet we have so many scientists within our midst, from the physical and mechanical sciences, to those sciences of the mind and the spirit. In our traditional communities, spiritual scientists were highly valued. Through looking to our past and recovering those valuable paradigms which had been lost along the path, recovering those values and applying them to our future – we can seize a new destiny.

We can and must preserve these values that restore ourselves to greatness and serve as solid basis for Reparations. Our wise, experienced and esteemed Elders will serve as governance which has been missing for far, too long.

Keidi Awadu and Baba H.K. Khalifah at the Virginia farm

Building with the Intention of Sustainability

Hwe Mu Dua - Symbol of Examination and Quality Control

One of the primary motivations for this specific set of actions called forth in this edition of the Conscious Rasta Report is that the current system by which 10's of millions of Africans in America and other parts of the world is unsustainable. This has been described with significant detail in the report up to this point and obviously reams of data can be presented to further develop this theme. Therefore, at this point our primary intention is to point out areas in which our efforts will serve to resolve this tremendous problem toward the most positive outcome that our creative resourcefulness can accomplish.

I must emphasize our need to reduce our individual costs of living by collectivizing whenever possible. All of us need the basics of food, clothing, shelter, security and education, among other critical needs. The current system by which these are being consumed is depleting the larger group of critically needed capital resources which could be redirected into more desirable facets of our economy.

Food sustenance is one area where the amount of money being spent on the micro and macro scale could be better invested in a self-serving system. Recent news reports on the growth of the natural foods markets leave us with great hopes that we could similarly get great return on investment on our Kujichagulia Village food production projects. An inspiring and revealing article appeared in the *Los Angeles Times* on June 13, 2013 written by Tiffany Hsu. While the article contained several impressive data analyses showing that this is indeed a great area for growth, certain passages stood out which I wish to cite for your understanding:

> Wild Oats Markets Inc., the closed purveyor of organic and natural foods, is planning a comeback this year, potentially aided by local billionaire Ron Burkle.
>
> The company, which has been out of operation since 2007, now says on its website that it is "re-introducing" its brand, bringing beverages,

snacks, cereals, pasta and other goods to store shelves…

The trademark could cover a brand offering retail and online grocery store services, with features such as home delivery, phone-in orders, convenience store items and gasoline, according to the document. The application also described catering and take-out food services.

Burkle is no stranger to supermarket deals.

The magnate was the largest shareholder of Wild Oats when the brand was sold for $565 million to rival Whole Foods Market Inc. in 2007. Earlier in his career, Burkle handled leveraged buyouts of grocery chains such as Food 4 Less, Ralphs and Fred Meyer.

In 2011, Yucaipa was part of a consortium of investors that pumped $490 million in financing into the Great Atlantic & Pacific Tea Co., or A&P. The infusion allowed the Northeastern supermarket company, which owns the Pathmark chain, to emerge from Chapter 11 bankruptcy.

As consumers become more health-focused and body-conscious, food products deemed to be organic and natural are gaining traction…

On Sunday, Target Corp. launched its Simply Balanced line of 250 products made without artificial ingredients and largely sans genetically modified content…

Last spring, Berkeley-based organic food company Annie's Inc. went public, opening at $31.11 a share. The stock has since risen nearly

28%, closing Wednesday at $39.77 a share. So far this year, Whole Foods' stock is up nearly 12%.

These ideas regarding the viability of the full-service supermarkets sector, a $80 billion annual chunk of our own domestic consumption, is an area where we would be best to capture market share and convert it to economic viability and employment for our own people.   There are many other opportunities that we've identified which would be equally lucrative.

Jobs creation within and beyond our Kujichagulia Villages environment must include:

- Food, clothing, shelter, security and education – meeting the basics of sustenance for our group;

- Providing lifelines to each of the Villages for our self-developing urban collectives;

- Building sustaining communities independent of the mainstream energy and utilities grids.

- Assuring that travelers from our global family are taken care of when then are within our territories;

- Assuring that no families, children or imprisoned member of our group gets left behind as we progress.

A New Self-Determining Economy: 18 Functions for a Kujichagulia Village

Dwennimmen - Symbol of Humility Together with Strength

Over the years, and during thousands of deep conversations, we have discussed in detail how we can enjoin great wealth development by doing for self. The following 110 ideas have all been explored in varying levels of in-depth engagement. I have divided them into 18 broad categories. In the years that have followed the original publication of the book, some of the following have been exploited, while others remain merely strong visions of what we could and should be doing. I challenge you to imagine the possibilities.

1. De-Urbanized Survival Zones with Housing

a. Escape from Constant Pressure Encouraging Unconscious Consumerism

b. Reconnecting our Fractured Psyches from Isolation to Community

c. Haven for Pregnant Women At-Risk

d. Rescuing our Young Males from Urban Killing Zones

e. A Place for Young Families to Homestead

f. Reducing the Overwhelming Expenses of Urban Housing

g. Escape from Big City Stress and Anxiety

h. Recovering Agricultural Lands Lost Over the Past Century

i. Combating Urban Homelessness

j. Functional Reparations Centers

2. Elderly Retirement Villages

a. Tapping the Wisdom of the Elders

b. The Council of Elders as Leadership

c.   Low-Cost Retirement Housing

d.   Advanced Residential Health Care for Residents

e.   Section 8 Housing Expense Support

f.   Insurance Policies Bequeathed to the Village

g.   Timeshare Housing

h.   Housing for the Elderly Scholars

3. Healing Retreats

a.   Chronic Disease Abatement

b.   Yoga and Qi Gong Classes

c.   Gourmet Raw Food and Vegan Cuisine

d.   Massage and Energy Therapy

e.   Weekend Health Seminars and Workshops

f.   Detoxification Facilities

g.   Weekly Healthy Potluck Feast

h.   Exercise and Fitness Training

4. Campground Facilities

a. Weekend Camping

b. Group Retreats

c. Leadership Training Intensive Workshops

d. Survival Training and Emergency Preparedness

e. Crisis Housing During Natural Disasters

f. Outdoor Kitchen and Dining Facilities

g. HBCU College Student Reunions (Spring Break)

5. Organic Food Production

a. In-House Consumption & Clinical Nutrition

b. Farmers' Market

c. Partnership with Urban Retailers

d. Training in Raised Bed Techniques

e. Fruit and Nut Orchards

f. Seedlings and Heirloom Seeds for Distribution

g. Composting for In-House Utilization and Marketing for Community Gardens

h. Aquaculture – Growing Fish and Sea Vegetables

i. Sprouting Organic Foods

6. Food Preservation and Packaging

a. Dehydrating and Packaging for Distribution

b. Canning and Food Distribution

c. House Label for Wholesale and Retail

d. Bulk Purchase of Consumables and Repackaging for Our Own Markets

e. Domestic Distribution of Imported Goods from Africa and Other Diaspora Producers

7. Healing Herbs Growing and Packaging

a. Growing Culinary Herbs for In-House Use

b. Supplying Medicinal Herbs to Practitioners

c. Branding Our Own Products for Online and Retail Distribution

8. Vocational Training Facilities

a. Holiday Arts and Crafts

b. Construction Trades

    i. Mobile work crew

    ii. Pre-fab housing units

a. Woodcraft and Furniture Making

    i. *Sukaka Mesa* (Kiswahili for "feast table") custom designed outdoor furniture

a. Sewing, Quilting, Knitting and Crochet

b. Doll Making & Cultural Toys and Games

c. Photography

d. Video Media Production

e. Craft Workshops for Independent Artists

f. Culinary Arts Training Academy

g. Sports and Fitness Training

9. **Convention Center**

a. Meeting Hall

b. Banquet Facility

c. Webcasting Capacity

10. Outdoor Amphitheater

a. Concerts

b. Lectures

c. Seasonal Galas and Celebrations

11. Agri-Tourism

a. Animal Husbandry

b. Tractor Rides

c. Work on the Farm Barter Exchange

d. Learning the Basics of Food Self-Sufficiency

e. Aquaculture (Fish Farming)

12. Eco-Tourism

a. Nature Walks

b. Plant Identification Training

c. Workshops on Permaculture and Sustainable
Living

d. Meditation Gardens

e. Labyrinth

13. Green Economy Home Construction & Training

a. Carpentry

b. Masonry and Foundation

c. Plumbing

d. Electrical

e. Roofing

f. Drywall and Painting

g. Landscaping

14. Sound Stage for Media Production

a. Online radio broadcast

b. Internet Protocol Television (IPTV)

c. Independent Film Production

d. Editing Stations

e. Music Production Studio

f. Film Festival

15. A People's University

a. Non-Traditional Education for Youth and Adults

b. Home Schooling Curriculum

c. Remote Learning Through the Internet

d. Youth Mentoring with Successful Adults

e. Field Laboratory for Research and Development

16. Sustainable Energy Development & Training

a. Solar Energy Installation and Generation

b. Wind Energy Installation and Generation

c. Biofuel Manufacturing

d. Permaculture and Organic Farming

e. Composting and Waste Management

17. Writers' Workshops and Book Production

   a. Annual Writers Retreat and Awards

   b. Editing and Ghost Writing Services

   c. Book Formatting and New Author Coaching

   d. Printing Facilities

   e. Alternative Media Production for Authors

18. Cultural Tourism

   a. Museums

   b. Research Library

   c. Country Marketplace

   i. Books, DVD's & Audios

   ii. Restaurant

   iii. Preserved Foods

   iv. Arts and Crafts

   v. Fashion Products

   a. Traditional Holiday Celebrations

vi.   Kwanzaa, Juneteenth, Birth Anniversaries,
       Harvest Festivals, Mardis Gras, African National
       Holidays, Holocaust Commemoration, etc.

   d. Spiritual Center

   i.   Worship Center Services

   ii. Meditation Garden

   iii. Training for African Centered Spiritual Systems

   iv. Marriage Ceremonies

   v.   Rites of Passage and Naming Ceremonies

   a. Honoring the Great Ancestors

Time Has Come to Launch Our Survival Arks

War Hor - Symbol of Vigilance to Sound a Battle Cry

1. Reparations Center for Research and Advocacy

2. Camping retreats

3. Organic food and herbs

4. Honoring of the Ancestors

5. Senior residences

6. Scholar retirement facilities

7. Permaculture training labs

8. Conference center

9. Mobile development force/ construction crew

10. Recruiting road trips with RV's

11. Construction warehouse with prefab housing

12. Arts & crafts workshops

13. Health spa

14. Youth training camps

15. Education system with remote learning youth and adults

16. Media production center with sound stage

17. Amphitheater

18. Young pregnant women's residence

19. Library

20. Counter the imprisonment for men and families

21. In house science laboratories

22. Sports, exercise and game facilities

23. Hiking trails and nature training

24. Aquaculture growing fish and sea vegetables

25. Investor club

26. Timeshare housing

27. Non-polluting transportation

28. Language immersion

29. Cultural education academies

30. Way station for continental African travelers

31. Refuge in times of emergency

32. Emergency preparedness and wilderness survival training

33. Martial arts training

Summary

I have debated as to how much time to spend filling in details for each of these economic suggestions. I have concluded that the best means of filling in such details would be engaging in community forums and workshops. I personally have engaged in nearly every one of these avenues listed. Undoubtedly, personal experience would come as quite practical. As Malcolm X instructed, "By any means necessary," we must bring these strategic ideas to fruition.

Addendum 2017 / 6257

Why wait? Why put off this critical mission for another year, a month, week or even another day? There is a Chinese proverb which states, "**The best time to plant a fruit tree is twenty years ago. The second-best time is now.**" Looking back at the twists and turns, rising hopes and downfalls, victories and abuses that we have endured since the culmination of the Civil Rights Struggle era, we most likely would like to have done many things differently for the ultimate benefit of the group.

Today, the body of informed literature which would be needed to restore and revitalize our communities has never been more prolific or more precise. There are countless scholars, within and without our ethnic group, whose works would enlighten our Golden Pathway toward sustained development.

Our relationship to national groups of people of African heritage around the globe has benefited immensely because of breakthroughs in technology, communications, the lowered cost of travel and increased access to institutions of power.

Without question, we are in better position to secure long-term empowerment today than at any other time during the past 500 years of our Maafa journey.

It is time that greater numbers of us step up and assume primary responsibility for the fate of our race. You are one of those called to such vanguard action; this I know because you have read this book thus far. From this point onward our actions must be more precise, collaborative, well-advised, timely and highly engaged. Across a broad spectrum of background developments, the time for a global African renaissance has never been better today than it has been in the past 1000 years.

Dare to be bold. Make a profound impact on your community, the larger society and the world. Be a major supplier of what the world needs for the century ahead. Stand out from the crowd and manifest the leader within that you've always envisioned would be your greatest potential. A suitable place to begin is within this transforming vision we call *Kujichagulia Villages*. Power, permanent and all-encompassing, is directly connected to land acquisition and development toward sustainable productivity.

I look forward to working alongside you on this great and noble task. Our mission is blessed by the Creator and sanctified by the tremendous sacrifices of countless numbers of our Beloved Ancestors. Having come to comprehend the amazing pathway upon which we have discovered ourselves, let us just simply get to the tasks which are immediately ahead.

Africa Rising… We got next!